learn to SPEAK DANCE

➤➤ *a guide to* CREATING, PERFORMING & PROMOTING ⇢ **YOUR MOVES** ⇇

WRITTEN BY ANN-MARIE WILLIAMS
DESIGN & ILLUSTRATIONS BY JEFF KULAK

Owlkids Books Inc.
10 Lower Spadina Avenue, Suite 400, Toronto, Ontario M5V 2Z2
www.owlkids.com

Parents and Guardians: Please use your own discretion when deciding if the pieces mentioned in the step-by-step guides are appropriate for your children.

Library and Archives Canada Cataloguing in Publication

Williams, Ann-Marie, 1979-

      Learn to speak dance : a guide to creating, performing, and promoting your moves / Ann-Marie Williams, Jeff Kulak.

Includes index.

Issued also in electronic format.

ISBN 978-1-926818-88-7 (bound).--ISBN 978-1-926818-89-4 (pbk.)

      1. Dance--Juvenile literature. I. Kulak, Jeff, 1983- II. Title.

GV1596.5.W55 2011   j792.8   C2011-900259-0

Library of Congress Control Number: 2010943321

E-book ISBN: 978-1-926818-15-3

Design and illustration: Jeff Kulak

  **Canada Council for the Arts**   **Conseil des Arts du Canada**   **ONTARIO ARTS COUNCIL** **CONSEIL DES ARTS DE L'ONTARIO**

We acknowledge the financial support of the Canada Council for the Arts, the Ontario Arts Council, the Government of Canada through the Canada Book Fund (CBF), and the Government of Ontario through the Ontario Media Development Corporation's Book Initiative for our publishing activities.

Manufactured by WKT Co. Ltd.
Manufactured in Shenzhen, Guangdong, China in March 2011
Job # 10CB3835

A   B   C   D   E   F

 **Publisher of Chirp, chickaDEE, and OWL**
www.owlkids.com

For L.S.—A.M.W.

For my sister, Kara—J.K.

LEARN TO SPEAK DANCE

GET A MOVE ON!

Have you ever seen a dancer so good—so fast, so balanced, almost floating on air—that you were just blown away? It's almost enough to make you believe the dancer is superhuman.

So, what's that "wow" factor all about, anyway? I mean, these dancers have got the same old bodies we all do, yet they can make them do such cool stuff. And they make it look so easy, too! That's got to feel amazing! And you know what? It does.

But, here's the thing—the world of dancing isn't some stuffy academy or impossibly cool VIP room that you can't get into. It's an everyday place—one that you and I live in. And those dizzy headspins, slick shuffles and ridiculously elegant pirouettes? You, too, have this power.

Sure, you won't become a master mover without putting in the time, but there's nothing stopping you from getting going. You know how soccer's so popular because all you need is a ball? Well, with dance, you already have everything you need—your body! So whether you want to dip a toe into the dance world, or just dive right in... *Let's go!*

So who's this self-professed dancing queen, anyway?

OK, so you've figured out that I'm really into dance. Ever since I was a kid, I spent a lot of time learning how to dance just because it was always way more fun than everything else. I loved putting on shows in my backyard, and lived for my dance recitals. Eventually, I liked it so much I decided to study it at university. I practiced and studied a lot and earned a few degrees, but also made sure there was lots of time to make dances and perform them with my friends at festivals and events. These days, I run a dance school so I can pass on all my favorite things about dance to a new generation. That's you!

CHAPTER 1

Dance It Out!

You're sitting nervously at your desk doing some last-minute cramming, when your teacher makes an announcement—your test is canceled. Yes! You're so relieved, you can't help flying out of your seat and jumping around with excitement. This is awesome!

You probably didn't think about it, but you were dancing. In fact, the fun of expressing how you feel with your body is exactly what dance is all about. It's the only time we humans move around just because it feels good, instead of with a goal in mind, like kicking a ball or running to the finish line. It just feels great to dance out whatever is going on inside our heads.

When you think about it this way, you already know how to dance. OK, so you can't do those killer breakdance moves you see on TV, but hear me out! Dance is just a mash-up of everyday movement and your imagination. A musician might learn to play piano or guitar, but a dancer's instrument is the human body. All you have to do is explore the one-of-a-kind artistic voice inside your instrument.

So celebrate and throw yourself a dance party for one. Shut your bedroom door, crank up your favorite tunes, and shake it like a Polaroid picture. Don't overthink how you should move, and don't judge yourself. You can't be wrong, so just do what feels good!

See? You are a dancer.

WHY WE DANCE

Even if you were a bit nervous, it probably felt pretty good when you and your friends hit the floor at your school dance. Well, there's a reason for that. Dancing tells your brain to release chemicals called endorphins that actually make you feel happier. Endorphins are like nature's mood lifter, and they're at work when you do stuff like laugh really hard or eat something you really love, like chocolate.

ALL TOGETHER NOW

When you feel that good, you want to share the love. That's why dancing is almost always involved when there's something to celebrate, like a wedding or a party. Dancing together is kind of like a big group hug, because it makes us feel closer to each other. It reminds us that we belong to a group, and that's a powerful feeling.

MAKING CONNECTIONS

Dancing creates togetherness between people, even total strangers. Jumping around at a concert creates an instant sense of belonging between hundreds of fans, while watching a ceremonial dance can connect you to an entire nation. Dance can be a link to the past—folk dancers have moves that are passed down through many generations. Around the world, people dance together to give thanks, prepare for battle, or say goodbye to a loved one.

STAND OUT

Dance may unify us, but it can also be a way to stand out from the crowd. Some people make up their own moves as a way of expressing what's unique about them. Whether you show off your signature style at parties or perform it on a stage, dance can be a way of presenting your ideas, just like a writer with a story.

Let It Out

Dance can mean lots of different things to different people. But deep down, we all love to express ourselves.

> 66 When I'm dancing I feel like I am sharing a part of myself. I feel free and happy. Sometimes I'm playing a character, and sometimes I'm just interpreting the music, but either way I am transported to a different place. 99
>
> —Heather Ogden
> **PRINCIPAL DANCER,**
> *NATIONAL BALLET OF CANADA*

WHAT'S IN A DANCE

When you break it down, every dance you see or do has a magic four-part formula that makes it tick:

BODY + SPACE + FORCE + TIME = DANCE

We call these the elements of dance. How you bring these elements together is what makes one dance unique from all the others.

THE BARE BONES

Every dance move starts with a body part—could be your head, could be your arms or legs. Whatever the body part, you can do all sorts of things with it—stretch it, sway it, twist it, swing it, hop on it, you name it!

SPACE EXPLORER

Now you need to put your move into space. No, I don't mean flying to the moon, I'm talking about the space all around you and the pathways you make in it while dancing. If you could leave footprints everywhere you went, what kind of patterns would you want to make? Straight lines? Twisty curves?

DYNAMIC MOVES

Some dances are soft and airy, while others pack a harder punch. These dances play with dynamics such as weight (heavy/light) and attack (sharp/smooth) to define their style.

JABBAWOCKEEZ
AMERICA'S BEST DANCE CREW SEASON 1

These guys mix up sharp and smooth moves with lots of quick stops to create their signature hip-hop style.

MARIUS PETIPA & LEONID IVANOV
CYGNETS DANCE FROM SWAN LAKE

A ballet classic, these swans are famous for their effortlessly light and flowing moves. Their pointe shoes help create the illusion of weightlessness.

HI HAT
HOW SHE MOVE

Step dancers use sharp and heavy moves to pound out their rhythms. It's definitely the flip side of ballet.

USE THE FORCE

Dancers sometimes call this dynamics, and you use it all the time without realizing it. Take walking. If you're bummed out, you slouch and shuffle around as though your body weighs a ton. But, if you're really excited, your steps are naturally light and bouncy. Changing the dynamics can give the same basic movement a totally new personality.

TIME TO ADD THE BEAT

Whether it's Beyoncé or Beethoven, all dances move to a beat. That's the steady pulse in a song that you can snap your fingers to. We really respond to rhythms—fast ones excite us, while slow ones calm us down. Even if there's no music, your dance creates its own rhythm, just like your body does with its heartbeat and breath, which are natural rhythms.

behind THE moves

You're watching in total awe as amazing dancers backflip, leap, and twist their bodies in ways that seem to defy gravity. Awesome, but how do they do it? What are you actually asking your body to do when you dance, anyway? No matter the style, every dancer works hard to get these basic dance principles right.

FINDING BALANCE

One day, you're on and can hold that one-footed upside-down pose forever. The next day, you can't stop falling over. Pretty frustrating, but trying to fight it just makes it worse. Instead of bullying your balance, you've got to relax to find it. Dancers call it "feeling grounded or centered." It feels a bit like being perfectly placed between two forces—one pulling you away from the Earth and the other pulling you toward it—like your body is working in harmony with gravity for a few fleeting moments.

JUST BREATHE

For dancers, breathing is more than just a way to get oxygen into your lungs—it's a way to bring life to your moves. When we're nervous, we hold our breath, which makes our movements look robotic and lifeless. Good dancers know how to extend the rise and fall of their breath like waves through all their movements. Some people think understanding breath is what makes the difference between a good technical dancer and a great artist. You can really see it when you watch slow, graceful dances like ballet—check out how the moves tend to grow and then shrink, just like your lungs as you breathe.

SPIN IT

Whether it's a breakdancer's head spin or a ballerina's pirouettes, turning is totally impressive to watch. If balance and breath are mysterious, turning is all about cold hard momentum. Ever tried to spin a penny on a table? The more force you give it, the faster and longer it spins. Dancers practice pushing off the floor and throwing their weight around to get more momentum. Once you've got that going, it's about finding a balanced position to let all that force spin you around. It's a pretty cool rush to give your body over to gravity like that.

MAKE THE LEAP

When some dancers jump, it's like they get higher, hover longer and come down slower than the rest of the world. No camera tricks or hidden trampolines here—just hours and hours of old-fashioned practice. Gravity-defying jumps come from seriously strong muscles, and a good understanding of how to use your *plié* (say it: plee-ay), or knee bend, to push off the floor. When you're jumping higher than you ever have before, all that practice is literally helping you reach new heights.

music & movement

Simply put, dancing to music is using your body to express what you are hearing. But how do we know how to do that?

What is it in each song that tells us how to move? Turns out, we humans are hardwired to do this. It's so instinctual, even babies dance long before they have a clue what they're doing. There are lots of scientists studying the brain, trying to figure out exactly why we react to music in this way. It's still a mystery, but here are a few key things we really react to. Check 'em out.

RHYTHMS WITHIN YOU

Above all else, we respond to a song's rhythm. No dance training required—we naturally speed up or slow down in sync with the song's tempo. We even stress the downbeat or accent in a rhythm by using stronger body movements.

100% NATURAL

Your heartbeat and your breath create two rhythms that are constants in your life. You use them to interpret other rhythms. That's why the sound of ocean waves is calming—it's about the same speed as your breathing when you're sleeping.

MUSICAL MOVES

These moves were made to physically dance out all the different sounds going on in the music.

DAFT PUNK
AROUND THE WORLD

CHOREOGRAPHY:
MICHEL GONDRY & BLANCA LI

Each group of bizarrely costumed dancers represents a different instrument in the song, creating a very cool visual effect.

IGOR STRAVINSKY
FROM THE BALLET
THE RITE OF SPRING

CHOREOGRAPHY:
VASLAV NIJINSKY

Back in the day, no one was ready for moves that pounded out such crazy rhythms. They were so unusual, the audience even rioted in their seats.

THE NICHOLAS BROTHERS
FROM THE MOVIE
STORMY WEATHER

CHOREOGRAPHY:
THE NICHOLAS BROTHERS

Watch how these rhythm geniuses play with the music—sometimes matching it perfectly with their taps, other times filling the silences like a game of copycat!

MOVING MELODIES

Know how songs can make people cry? (Not you, of course!) A song's melody sends messages to your brain that trigger your emotions and affect the way you move. It's automatic—put on a peppy song, you'll naturally want to bounce around. But turn up that horror movie theme, and you can't help creeping about. Dancers use these reactions to their advantage by exaggerating them in their performances. When someone does this well, we say they danced with a lot of "feeling."

VOLUMIZER

Musicians use dynamics (moving between loud and quiet sounds) the same way that dancers use force (moving between strong and soft moves). So it's no wonder that dancers can interpret musical dynamics without missing a beat! For the most part, we translate loud sounds with bigger, punchier actions, and quiet sounds with softer, gentler moves.

DANCE DANCE EVOLUTION

Have you ever thought about what makes a dance style? It's kind of like fashion or slang, but for your body. You're probably into similar clothing as your friends, or you have your own phrases that make your parents wonder what you're talking about. These common things become your group's style. They express who you are to the world. It happens on the dance floor too! Just like a new fashion trend, when enough people like the same moves, a dance style is born.

TRENDSETTERS

Love dancing to a hip-hop beat, but also dig the Ukrainian dance classes you've been taking since you were small? No need to pick just one style—mixing up styles is how dance continues to grow. In fact, many of the styles we know and love are already fusions. Jazz dance started as a combo of ballet and African, and over time picked up moves from modern dance, breakdance and even acrobatics.

ON THE MOVE

Every time you bust a move, you are a part of the evolution of dance. By choosing to do a move you think is cool, you're casting your vote on how a dance style should grow and change. Bit by bit, person by person, the style evolves— sometimes in different ways all over the world. Take breakdance, for example. Today, there are huge international competitions where each country shows off its unique type of breaking.

CHANGE IT UP

Sometimes dance is more than just fun. It can also be a way of protesting, or challenging something you don't like. Have you ever seen an old rock 'n' roll film from the 50s of teenagers doing the twist? It might look pretty corny by today's standards, but back then the twist looked totally wild compared to their parents' ballroom dancing. It was a teenager's way of saying, "I'm doing things my way." Rock on!

Mixmaster

Nova's a choreographer whose personal style is a blend of modern steps and a classical Indian style called bharatanatyam.

> ❝ I don't think of it so much as mixing styles, but more as being true to myself. I studied bharatanatyam in Canada, I am influenced by the diversity of artistic practice in Toronto. I think of it as taking my bharatanatyam tool box and building a contemporary house. ❞
>
> —*Nova Bhattacharya*
> **CHOREOGRAPHER**

CHAPTER 2

I Think I Can...

Yep, it feels great to set your inner dancer free and just do what comes naturally. I highly recommend busting a move to let loose on a regular basis, but this is very different than learning a style of dance with specific steps and poses.

OK, it's true. Dancing may be natural, but every style has its own rules for how to move that take time to master. That's why becoming a great dancer takes lots of practice. Fortunately, dancing is also energizing, exciting and super fun to do, which means that learning new moves always feels more like a good time than hard work.

There are so many ways for you to participate in the world of dance. Everything from shaking your body alone in your room to dance clubs, classes, and crews. You just need to feel comfortable enough to take that first step in the right direction.

And where exactly does that step lead? It's different for everyone, but think of it this way: All awesome dancers you see today started at the same beginning as you—tripping and stumbling their way through some basic steps. Oops. Bit by bit, they got a little better, until one day, their bodies were tossing out super-cool moves with the same ease that you tie your shoes.

So, who wants to get started? Just put one foot in front of the other and follow me...

Most people with a dancing bug start out in the privacy of their own living rooms. It takes a lot of guts to throw yourself into a dance class or group, so it's pretty normal to want to find your groove on your own first.

WATCH AND LEARN

Imitating dance videos is a hugely popular way to learn, and people everywhere have been doing it since they were invented. There's nothing amateur about it, either. It'll help you learn to "pick up" or copy steps quickly, an important skill all the pros need in order to nail an audition or keep up in a fast-paced class. But in the beginning, start slow and break the dance into bite-sized pieces. Copy a few moves, hit stop, and rewind and repeat them until they feel familiar in your body. Bit by bit, you'll learn the whole thing.

MIRROR, MIRROR ON THE WALL

Part of learning to dance is watching yourself in action. That's why dance studios have big mirrors. Once you're got a few moves under your belt, try them out in front of a mirror, or better yet, film yourself and watch it back. You'll start to notice little things that don't quite match the moves in the video—maybe that arm move needs to be sharper or bending your knees more there will look even cooler. Don't be too hard on yourself if you look clumsy—learning takes time!

NAME THAT STEP

So you're ready to admit you've mastered the dance from that Rihanna video. Nice! Did you know that each of those moves you learned has a name and rules for how to do them properly? Whether it's breakdance or ballet, each style has its own technique made up of basic positions, steps, and ways of moving. They are like the building blocks for making dances. If you're ready to dig a little deeper into your favorite style, there are loads of instructional videos online and at your local library where you can begin.

Break the Mold

Many dancers out there are self-taught. All you really need to get going is the will.

66 I never really had a teacher or mentor teach me how to dance, but I did have a lot of support from close friends and family. I think we are all dancers inside, so whenever you feel it, just turn on some music and let your body go. 99

—B-boy Luca "Lazylegz" Patuelli
ILLMASK & ILL-NABILITIES CREW

Dancing
WITH A
Partner

Great dance partners can always impress us with their effortlessly coordinated moves as they glide across the floor. But if you've ever tried dancing with a partner, you know that it's hard enough to figure out your own steps, let alone sync them up with someone else's! Partner dancing is like a conversation between two people where words are replaced with touch and movement. The more you get to know and trust your partner, the smoother your moves will be.

FOLLOW THE LEADER

There are lots of different dance styles that involve partnering, including ballroom, salsa, and swing. Even though there are basic steps, partners improvise their order and direction on the spot. To make this work there's always one lead, who makes the decisions, and one follower, who has to be ready for anything! This forces you to be in the moment—if you hesitate, you'll slow down your partner, and if you anticipate, you may guess wrong about where your partner's going.

DYNAMIC DUOS

When two partners hit the stage, we call it a duet (or *pas de deux* in ballet). They don't have to use the lead/follow system because all the steps are rehearsed in advance. They've worked out all the kinks like how hard to lean during that pose, or how much force is needed to lift into that leap. During a performance, they can immediately feel if something is a little off and needs to be adjusted. Some partners even talk to each other through hidden physical cues that the audience can't see. As in that double hand squeeze means "we're going for the big lift at the end."

GET SQUARE

Some styles take partner dancing to the next level by adding group formations into the mix. Take square dancing, which is making an underground revival right now with young people everywhere. In it, four couples dance together, exchanging partners and weaving around each other. Turns out, our grandparents really knew how to have fun with each other on the dance floor!

STEP *by* STEP

TWO TO TANGO

These dance styles are all about perfect partnering and fancy footwork.

SWING KIDS
FROM THE MOVIE *SWING KIDS*
CHOREOGRAPHY: OTIS SALLID

Swing dancing was all about letting loose with a partner to some great live jazz music. Rebelling from the stricter rules of ballroom, swing dancers mixed in their own steps and personalities, as seen in this movie.

DANCING CHEEK TO CHEEK
FROM THE MOVIE *TOP HAT*
CHOREOGRAPHY: HERMES PAN

Fred Astaire and Ginger Rogers are perhaps the most celebrated dance partnership of all time, so check out how they glide effortlessly through each move in perfect sync with each other.

TANGO
FROM THE MOVIE *TAKE THE LEAD*

Even though this dance is slow, you've got to be 100% in tune with your partner to make it look this polished and passionate.

Physical Feats

Each dance style has its own rules, and every move has a purpose. Here's a basic rundown of what different body parts can do on the dance floor.

HEAD

Your head is often the last thing you think about when dancing, and rookie dancers are often caught staring at the floor. Your face is the most expressive part of your body, so ham it up a bit and use it to accentuate the vibe of your moves, be it happy, strong, or silly.

RIB CAGE

The dance world is really divided on this one. Some styles—like ballroom or Irish step dance—say the ribs should stay still, poised, and upright. But others are all about big, bold chest moves— think of African dancers or b-boys popping, when they move their chest with quick jerky motions.

ARMS

Your arms generally extend the moves that start at the core, or center, of your body. Whether you're going for graceful arm swings or aggressive punches, a good trick to bring lots of energy and reach into your arms is to imagine beams of light coming from your chest and extending through your fingertips.

HIPS

For some dance styles, like salsa and belly dance, the hips are the center of all movement. They dance out the rhythm and create moves that ripple through the whole body.

KNEES

Your knees are one of the most important instruments in dance. You've probably heard the word *plié* before, which means bend. Knee bends are worth perfecting because they act like springboards—they provide the strength and momentum needed to do all those amazing leaps, as well as a nice soft cushion for landing.

FEET

Some dance styles, like tap and step dancing, are all about fancy footwork. They train the tiny muscles of the feet to move with quick precision. Those little muscles also help a lot to keep you balanced in hard poses, so imagine they have roots growing down into the ground.

TAKE THE LEAP

Whether it's taking a class or forming a group, teaming up with others is the best way to grow as a dancer. Not only is it a real thrill to be in a group of dancers all doing the same moves at the same time, but you'll learn faster, too.

CLASS ACT

If you're the studious type, joining a class is the most obvious way to learn. There are lots of dance studios out there, so take some time to find a teacher you click with. A great teacher will not only inspire you and show you new steps, but also help you discover your inner confidence and strength. Most schools will let you try a class for free, so you can shop around, and if money's tight, some schools may let you do volunteer work in exchange for class.

AROUND TOWN

If a structured class isn't for you, scope out more relaxed ways to get dancing. Maybe there is a dance club at your school, or a b-girl crew in your neighborhood that you totally admire. Or why not get in touch with your heritage by joining a traditional dance club at your community center? Once you look around, you'll notice all sorts of places where people can dance and learn from each other.

DO IT YOURSELF

B-boys and b-girls call it their "crew." To modern dancers, it's their "company" or "collective." Whatever word you and your friends use, it's all the same thing—your own dance group! This is your chance to go DIY, hang with some friends, and create a dance vision all your own. And since you call the shots, there's also a little less pressure—you can improve at your own pace.

A Teacher's Gift

It doesn't happen everyday, but sometime you might come across a teacher that blows you away, and helps you see potential for yourself you never knew you had.

> **66** I always wanted to become an actress until my first movement class led by a teacher named Patricia Beatty. From the moment I saw all the ways she could move—from a panther, to a blossoming flower, to a coiling spring—I understood I would be a dancer. **99**
>
> —*Peggy Baker*
>
> **PEGGY BAKER DANCE PROJECTS,**
> *FAMOUS CONTEMPORARY DANCER*
> *AND CHOREOGRAPHER*

START IT UP

A dance group can form just to create a single piece, or it can stay together for years and years. No matter how long they last, great groups can grow from humble beginnings, and while your moves get stronger, so will your friendships.

STRENGTH IN NUMBERS

When it comes to dance making, more heads are better than one. You'll be amazed at all the cool moves you'll come up with that you'd never have dreamed up on your own. Everyone's excitement will feed the group. That helps you build your confidence and take on bigger shows.

WHO'S WITH ME?

When you're looking for dancers, go for enthusiasm over talent, at least in the beginning. You want people who are equally excited about improving their dance moves, otherwise they might get bored and bail on you after a few weeks.

SPACE TO CREATE

Every group needs a practice space, and that's often someone's basement or living room when you first start out. If that's not doable, see if you can use your school gymnasium or theater. Last but not least, for a bit of money you can rent space at a local community center, church, or dance studio. Make sure they have discount rates for young people and students.

66 It took about a year to develop our teamwork and chemistry as a crew. Now we battle all around the world, and learn a lot from traveling and training with other dancers who share their knowledge. 99

—B-boy Drops (a.k.a Jon Reid)
SUPERNATURALZ CREW

The perfect dance studio

You don't need much to get dancing, but if you're shopping around for a space, here are a few things to consider:

Floors—they're not all created equal. Hard, cold floors like concrete are tough on your joints, so look for wood or rubber (like in some school gyms). Dance studios have sprung floors, which is just like it sounds—little springs installed under the floor to help soften your landings.

Mirrors are a bonus so you can see what you're doing in real time.

A sound system helps so you won't have to lug a stereo back and forth to every practice.

All Together Now

"I don't want to use that song!"
"That step? At the finish? Are you nuts?!"

It's inevitable: when creating something as a group, not everyone is going to agree. But if you can keep your cool and remember it's all part of the process, you can stop little disagreements from turning into wars.

CREATIVE CRITICISM

When you're not crazy about someone else's step, blurting out a negative comment will only bruise their ego and start a fight. Find a positive spin, like "How about we do this in a pyramid to give it a bit more bang?" If everybody else agrees with you, they'll immediately back you up. But, if they all think it's fine as is, you need to admit defeat and go with the flow.

NONSENSE WELCOME

Being respectful to your fellow dancers is not only the way to keep peace, but is also crucial to coming up with brilliant ideas. Try to create an open-minded atmosphere where even the most nonsensical ideas are welcome—that's where the best moves come from!

KNOW YOUR ROLE

The choreography's not done, the music needs to be edited, and no one booked the rehearsal space. Keep your group in order by dividing up what needs to get done. There's usually someone who's organized and wants to schedule rehearsals, or a creative keener who wants to come up with some new choreography before the next practice. Put that to use!

GOALS AND DEADLINES

Having a common goal will help unify your group. This could be making a dance for your next school assembly, or entering that amateur breakdance competition next month. Whatever it is, try and figure out how much you need to practice to reach that goal, and make sure everyone's cool and committed.

Auditions

It's bound to happen at some point in every dancer's life—the dreaded first audition. I'll bet you've seen one in a dance movie or on TV, where a bunch of mean-looking panelists scrutinize a group of terrified young dancers. In real life, those judges are actually encouraging, but it's still tough to put yourself out there like that.

WHAT TO EXPECT

Every audition runs a little differently, so find out as much as you can about it in advance. You may be asked to perform a dance you've prepared, or need to learn a new routine when you arrive. Check to see what to wear, and always show up early so you've time to warm up. You might also need to make a dance resume that lists your training and performance experience.

COOL, CALM, AND COLLECTED

When it's your turn to give it a go, treat it like a performance and give it all you've got. Remember that the "nasty judge" stereotype isn't real. They all started out in the same place as you! The more fun you have in your audition, the better you'll dance.

Pushing Past Nerves

Even experienced pros find auditioning scary. Over time, everyone finds their own tricks for calming their nerves.

> 66 I always get a little nervous before an audition. But, I tell myself that I can only do my best and remember that the panel wants you to succeed and get the job. 99
>
> —*Valerie Stanois*
> **MUSIC THEATER "TRIPLE THREAT"**
> *WE WILL ROCK YOU, ROCK OF AGES*

Confidence boosters!

Easier said than done? Here are some ways to put things in perspective:

· Every famous dancer has had many audition rejections. It's not only about talent—sometimes you just don't have the look a casting director is going for.

· One bad audition won't end a career. Most cool dance jobs come from friends calling you up and inviting you.

· It's true what they say—if you don't try, you won't succeed. Just treat each audition as useful training for the next time.

CHAPTER *3*

Making Dances

Ever read a book that was so good, you couldn't put it down? Great dances are the same way—there's something so captivating about how it's put together, your eyes just want to soak it all in.

Those dancers aren't just making that stuff up on the spot. Just like stories, dances are written with beginnings and endings and different sections in between. The writer is called a choreographer.

Being a choreographer is different from being a dancer. It's a skill all its own. A great performer may stand out in a dance show, but it's up to the choreographer to come up with the interesting moves in the first place—an important job! The best choreographers figure out how to put their personality into a dance. They spend years developing their own unique way of moving that sometimes creates an entirely new dance style! When that happens, they become an icon in the dance world, and their moves are copied all over.

Some dancers decide that choreography isn't for them, and that they'd rather focus on mastering moves or being an amazing performer. On the flip side, some choreographers never perform— they'd rather be behind the scenes coming up with incredible moves and watching them come to life on stage. That's good because like a great book, we're always ready to be amazed by new dances.

Follow THAT Song

Often, a dance begins with a song you like—and most of the time, that song finds you. You're out shopping or listening to the radio when something comes on that just gets inside you. It instantly makes you want to jump around, or conjures up quiet, faraway memories. Whatever the feeling, that's what people mean when they say a song "moved" them. It's like it's speaking directly to you, just asking to be choreographed.

GET CARRIED AWAY

Once you've found a song that moves you, dive into it and see where it takes you. Listen to all the different sounds going on and the cool ways they all work together. Maybe that awesome drumbeat makes you want to stomp your feet, while the vocals inspire some funny dreamy arm moves. Just start to let your body move however it wants to.

OUT OF ORDER

When it comes to making moves, you don't have to start at the beginning of the song. Focus in on the part in the music where it feels like your moves are coming out most naturally. Keep repeating that small section until you find yourself dancing the same actions over and over. That's where your first bits of choreography will come from. Eventually you'll have lots of them to move around and piece together like building blocks.

MAKE YOUR OWN RULES

Most songs have a basic structure with a few verses and a repeating chorus between them. Choreographers don't really have rules like that, but there are some ways that moves get grouped together and labeled:

Step—A step is a short series of moves that's only a few seconds long.

Phrase/Section—This is a longer combination of steps all strung together. It usually relates to a part of the music, like the intro or the chorus.

Transitions—A transition is the spot where one phrase meets another. You want to make them blend smoothly into each other.

Go With Your Gut

Discovering your first moves is more about feelings than logic, so don't over think it.

" I play the music over and over again, allowing it to become natural. The second I'm inspired to move, I just let go. At first, it's not about remembering what I did, more about the feeling it leaves. I call it playtime, and usually it's just as fun! **"**

—*Tré Armstrong*
FILM CHOREOGRAPHER,
HONEY, TURN THE BEAT AROUND
JUDGE, *SO YOU THINK
YOU CAN DANCE CANADA*

Inspiration!

Most choreography is made purely to "dance out" a great song. It's interesting to watch, and doesn't have to actually mean anything. But there are lots of things that inspire choreographers in addition to music. And sometimes, they turn everyday experiences and ideas into powerful dances with a message.

HAVE YOUR SAY

Many choreographers want their moves to tell a story. They'll get their dancers to act out a plot with movement instead of words. This is called narrative dance, and you can find it everywhere from classic ballets like *The Nutcracker* to the latest music videos. To make it work, you need to mix moves you love with everyday gestures that people understand, like pointing, marching, and waving.

MODERN MOVERS

Sometimes, the most inspiring thing to a choreographer is the human body itself. Many contemporary choreographers forget about stories, and focus solely on coming up with interesting shapes and patterns for the bodies in their dances. We call this "abstract choreography" because it's not supposed to look like or mean anything in particular. It just looks really cool.

FROM THE HEART

Have you ever seen a film about a big issue, like *An Inconvenient Truth,* that made you so mad you wanted to do something? Movies have a way of inspiring others like that, and some choreographers see dance in the same way. A themed dance can get people's attention and say, "Hey! This is important to me—and I think you should care about it, too."

DANCE OF CHANCE

Choreographer Merce Cunningham wasn't into telling stories, so he came up with chance methods for making dances. You may not have heard of him, but his work was a big influence on other choreographers. He would choose his steps by rolling some dice onto a big chart with options for body movements, pathways, dynamics, and tempo. What happens next? Let the dice decide!

STEP *by* STEP

STARTING POINTS

From stories to struggles, great dances are born from all sorts of ideas. Start seeing the world around you as potential inspiration.

MICHAEL JACKSON
THRILLER
CHOREOGRAPHY: MICHAEL PETERS

These dancing zombies are great, and their moves also help tell the story. This dance is so loved that people all over the world learn the moves, and perform them simultaneously to break world records.

POINTS IN SPACE
CHOREOGRAPHY: MERCE CUNNINGHAM

Here's Merce's famous "chance" choreography in action. For him, it was all about the unexpected dance discoveries that came from exploring random movement combos.

REVELATIONS
CHOREOGRAPHY: ALVIN AILEY

Ailey created this tribute to African-American cultural heritage because he was moved by the historic struggle for equality. Forty years later, this dance still touches audiences when it is performed around the world.

Make Your Own DANCE STEP

Every dance you see is a combination of the four elements: body, space, force, and time. Here's a game to help you choreograph your own step—it's kind of like Twister for dance. Whether your step ends up ridiculous, cool, or totally bizarre, the fun is in the trying!

BEFORE YOU START:

· Move the furniture to give yourself space.

· Grab some music, the more random the better.

· Find a mirror, or better yet, film your final step.

STEP 1

Choose a body part.

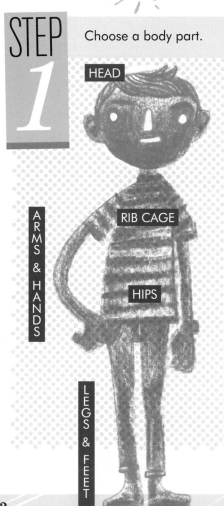

HEAD

ARMS & HANDS

RIB CAGE

HIPS

LEGS & FEET

STEP 2

Choose a move for that body part and try it out.

CIRCLE & TWIST

RISE & FALL

SWAY & SHAKE

STRETCH & BEND

STEP 3

Like it? It's time to make it travel! (Dance speak for moving from one spot to another.) Combine a traveling step with your move from step two.

WALKING

RUNNING

LEAPING

SLIDING

NO THANKS

I want my step to stay on the spot

STEP 4

Now add a pathway— a direction to travel through space.

IN A CIRCLE

DIAGONALLY IN A STRAIGHT LINE

RANDOM CURVY PATHWAYS

SIDEWAYS

STEP 5

Pick a song at random and try out your new step. Let the rhythm guide your speed and inspire changes like adding accents or pauses. Try out a few songs and choose the one you like best.

STEP 6

Dynamics add personality and feeling to your moves. I'll bet the music you picked already inspired you to move with certain qualities. See if you can figure out what they are, and then play around with some different ones. Try experimenting with these dynamics:

SMOOTH & FREE FLOWING

LIGHT & BOUNCY

SHARP & HEAVY

DONE! Have you found a winner? Why not make a few more steps and string them together for a longer combination? You can find inspiration for new steps all around you. Borrow some moves from music videos you like, and remix them using the elements.

Lead the Way

The choreographer is like the coach of a team, running rehearsals and teaching moves. You want to bring out the best in your dancers so you can collectively accomplish more than you could alone. This kind of leadership takes practice, but knowing how others do it can help you on your way.

TYPE A, TYPE B

Every choreographer finds his or her own approach to making steps in the rehearsal studio:

· The über-prepared type arrives on day one with a notebook documenting the entire dance. He or she acts more like a teacher, demonstrating the steps until the dancers learn them.

· Another type is a more intuitive choreographer, who throws out odd images like "be jellyfish at a disco" and asks the dancers to dream up moves on the spot.

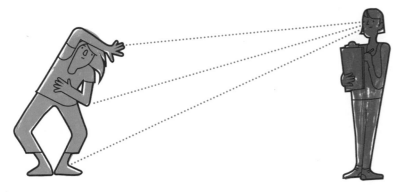

THE CHOREOGRAPHER'S EYE

Whatever approach you take, it's the choreographer's job to watch everything carefully and pick out the steps that look interesting. Your first job is to be hyper selective, and notice the little gems that have the potential to grow into cool-looking steps. Then you want to push and play with them to make them better, always watching for ways to improve them. That's the basic formula for building a great dance!

KEEPING TRACK

Even though you think you'll remember, by next week's rehearsal everything you've come up with may be totally out of your head. That's why you need to either make notes or record the final steps you've come up with. Writing down dance steps is a fun challenge—many choreographers end up inventing their own language to describe stuff. It's not unusual to hear one say, "OK dancers, let's do the monkey-slide-high-jump phrase and go right into the scatter-and-balloon-pop section!"

Positive Motivation

Teaching a bunch of new moves to a group can be tough on everyone. It helps to keep the mood light and fun.

> 66 I always have a good time when I choreograph. I'm super excited and that's contagious. I love to laugh and scream—it's just easier when you put your crew in a good mood. 99
>
> —Jean-Marc Généreux
> **BALLROOM DANCER & CHOREOGRAPHER,** *SHALL WE DANCE*
> **JUDGE,** *SO YOU THINK YOU CAN DANCE CANADA*

MUSCLE MEMORY

The first time most people try to learn choreography they become clumsy and slow, waiting for their puzzled brain to tell their body what to do next. But learning new steps is like riding a bike—practice enough, and suddenly you don't have to stop and think about it anymore. Dancers call this "muscle memory," and it's the secret to mastering new moves.

YOUR DANCING BRAIN

There was a time when you had to think really hard to push those bicycle pedals. Now muscle memory makes it second nature—your brain has wired itself to remember how to do it. Dance pushes your muscle memory to the extreme until eventually you can dance faster than you can think the steps through. Other professionals do it, too. That's how a soccer pro like Lionel Messi kicks the ball in the net without stopping to think about it, or a pianist's fingers fly quickly over the keys.

ONLY TEN YEARS TO GO!

Here's the deal—there's no way to rush your muscle memory. That's why they say it takes ten years to make a dancer...and why dance teachers get so serious about proper technique. As you practice seemingly simple exercises over and over, your brain hangs on to those movement patterns. Another reason to do it right from the start? It's much harder to unlearn a bad habit than to just do it right from the beginning. That's why lots of people can't stop bad habits like biting their nails.

THE BIG REWARD

Keep practicing, knowing that it will all pay off when you're up on stage and the steps will flow out of you as naturally as breathing. That's probably what's so awe-inspiring about watching an amazing dancer. In the back of our minds, we know that all the seemingly effortless grace and power comes from hours and hours of struggle, perseverance, and hard work. Just like an Olympic athlete, we can accomplish our goals through something as simple and straightforward as dedicated practice.

The Choreographer's Tool Box

Ever seen a flash mob video, when out of nowhere hundreds of people on the street start dancing in unison? We love it, but even good things get tired after a while, especially when there are so many other ways for a group to dance together!

To keep things interesting, play with the arrangement of your dancers—just like when musicians mix and match different combinations of instruments and sounds in their songs. You can use these classic tricks, or come up with your own ideas.

DO THE WAVE

Make a cool wave-like effect with a "canon." One person starts a step, and then the next dancer starts a few seconds later, then another, and another, until you get an awesome ripple-like look that's totally mesmerizing to watch.

FOLLOW THE LEADER

This one's actually called "call and response," and just like it sounds, it's when one dancer does a step, and then a second dancer or group repeats it right after.

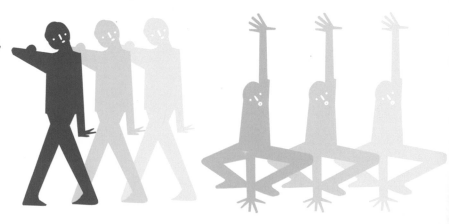

LITTLE CHANGES

If you've got a step you love, try repeating it a few times, but each time changing it up a bit. You can speed it up, change the dynamics from heavy to light, move it in a new direction, or anything else. The posh name for this is "theme and variation," and it's always a crowd pleaser.

REAL-LIFE KALEIDOSCOPES

Your dancers can make all kinds of shapes and patterns in space, so don't get stuck with everyone facing the front all the time. Try out some circles, triangles, or diagonal lines (just to name a few), and experiment with making steps that travel through space.

NUMBERS GAME

Generally, choreographers pull out the whole-group-dancing-in-unison step for the big bang moments of the dance. Create some quieter moments by sprinkling in some solos, duets, trios or other small groupings of performers. It'll make your dance more dynamic and add to the awesome power of steps in unison.

COMPOSITION

These guys used classic tools to make their own signature moves stand out.

OK GO
A MILLION WAYS
CHOREOGRAPHY: TRISH SIE

Our favorite internet dancers do it all! From unison into clever groupings and formation patterns, they even pack in some cute partnering. They show us that great moves don't have to be overly complicated.

BY A WATERFALL
FROM THE MOVIE
FOOTLIGHT PARADE
CHOREOGRAPHY: BUSBY BERKLEY

Watch past the two-minute musical introduction to get to some classic Hollywood dance magic. Busby was obsessed with geometric formations, and this aqua-dance is all about making beautifully elaborate patterns.

SOUND OF MUSIC
FLASH MOB AT CENTRAL STATION, ANTWERP BELGIUM

With over two hundred dancers, this shows us how irresistible unison dancing is to watch. It's just gets more powerful as people keep joining—the final group wave finishes it off with a bang!

Finishing Touches

If you hear someone say your dance "has legs," take it as a compliment.

It's a saying in the dance world to describe a piece that grabs your attention and keeps it all the way through. So what's the trick to finding your legs? Editing, and lots of it!

TRIM AWAY

Editing is like getting a haircut. You take away all the bits you don't need until your awesome new look emerges. In every rehearsal try to trim away, bit by bit, all the steps that don't look great. Don't save it all for the rehearsal before the big show, or you'll definitely run out of time.

RUN THROUGH

Once you've got a rough version of the dance, it's time to do a run-through. That's just a rehearsal where you do the dance from start to finish without stopping. It totally helps to film the dance, so you can study it later. Watch carefully and take note of all the really exciting steps. Don't be afraid to cut anything that looks like filler. A short dance full of great moves is way better than a long snoozer.

THE OUTSIDE EYE

Find a trusted friend and ask them for an honest opinion about your dance. Ask them to point out what they liked and if there were any parts that seemed too long or boring. This takes guts, because no one wants to be criticized, but it's way better to hear it from a friend than an audience. Besides, you'll discover that getting a chance to talk about your dance is actually really fulfilling.

ROOM TO GROW

No matter how much you edit, you'll never really hit a moment when the dance screams out "I am complete!" That's totally normal, so don't feel like you have to have it all figured out. Dances are always evolving with time and performances. Even the best choreographers in the world will tweak and change things after watching their dance performed, sometimes for years and years.

CHAPTER 4

Performing Live

It's almost show time. The sets are up, the costumes look great, and you know your steps by heart. The excitement between you and your fellow dancers is building. This is what all that hard work has been leading up to, right?

Getting on stage is a chance to make a statement and tell the world a bit about yourself—just like a storyteller. You want to invite your audience into your dance world and take them on a little journey. Since we don't get to do this every day, it's exciting to be the center of attention for a while. And yes, hearing an audience cheer and clap for the dance moves you've worked so hard to perfect feels pretty awesome!

Even if you're really shy, you just might love the rush of performing. Lots of dancers feel more comfortable dancing for hundreds of people than they do talking to a small group. But there are others who decide the stage is not for them, and that's cool, too. It doesn't stop them from dancing it up at parties, challenging themselves in their weekly tap class, or choreographing totally amazing dances behind the scenes.

The only way to find out whether you enjoy being on stage is to give it a go. When the music starts and the lights go up, you'll get to experience what many dancers describe as "being in the moment." Your body takes over and just knows what to do. The adrenaline pumping through you is making your moves feel bigger and stronger than ever before, and you're so focused that the rest of the world just seems to hover around you like in *The Matrix*. Worth trying, I think!

GET ON STAGE

If you've got the urge to get on stage, start looking for events to perform at, like your school talent show or the street fair in your neighborhood. Don't be afraid to ask if you can be involved—that's pretty much how everyone gets started. If you're super into it, you can put on your own show. It's a lot more work, but making a show from scratch means you get complete creative control. Oh, the power!

HOT SPOT

Maybe it's your backyard or a surprise performance in a shopping mall—when it's your show, you can get creative about where you want it to happen. Chances are, places like your school auditorium or a local cafe will work best for you, but dance shows have taken place just about everywhere. In fact, there's a whole group of "site specific" choreographers who seek out cool places and then design dances to fit them.

FILL THE BILL

Most first dances are between two and five minutes long. That's fine for a casual backyard show, but if you want a full evening event, you'll need more than that to keep 'em entertained. Why not team up with some friends and make it a variety show, or in dance-world speak, a "mixed bill." Bring in actors, jugglers, musicians, and whoever else to get something for everyone. Your audience will be bigger, and you'll be making friends who may invite you to their gigs in the future.

DO IT UP

If you want to, there are all sorts of extra bells and whistles you can add that will turn your dance piece into a full show experience. Round up all your creative pals to help out with everything from costumes and sound effects to totally hip, wall-worthy posters. You'll be amazed at all the cool ideas others will come up with that you'd never have thought up on your own.

Location, Location,

Some choreographers avoid the theater, using an unusual location to help create the right mood for their show.

66 I like to use spaces that are part of our everyday lives instead of theaters. Each space has its own distinct energy made up of its shapes, smells, lighting, and history. This adds meaning to the dance in ways that can't be found in a regular theater. 99

—Noémie Lafrance
CHOREOGRAPHER, *SENS PRODUCTIONS,*
FEIST'S "1234" VIDEO

55

SET the SCENE

It was a dark, stormy night... No wait, the sun was shining and the birds were chirping. The sights and sounds around us really affect our mood. Theater and film pros know this, and play with our senses through sets and special effects in movies and plays. Borrow some of their tricks and create the perfect ambiance for your show, too.

SET IT UP

Turn your backyard into a twilight oasis with blowing sheets and candles, or transform the community center stage into a graffiti alley with a spray-painted backdrop and some garbage can props.

Your set will transform your stage into the world you imagine your dance belongs in. Whether you want to go natural or sci-fi, minimal or over the top, think about the atmosphere you want your audience to experience. Start noticing cool spaces around you, and check out pictures for more inspiration. Sketch out some ideas on paper, and when you're ready, buy some supplies, order a pizza, and have a set-building party with your friends.

SHED SOME LIGHT

Ever told a ghost story with a flashlight under your chin? That story wouldn't have been half as creepy if you had told it in broad daylight. It's usually the last thing we think about when we watch a show, but lighting plays a huge role in setting a mood. There are all sorts of simple and cheap ways to get some cool lighting effects. Why not:

· Color a room with tinted light bulbs.

· Get spooky with glow-in-the-dark bracelets and paint.

· Make starlight by shining a flashlight into a retro disco ball.

· Create the classic strobe effect by turning the lights on and off as fast as you can.

· Work with nature's lighting and perform at sunset.

CUE SOUNDS

All day long, sounds affect our emotions—they can be subtle, like the calming sound of crickets at night, or overwhelming, like the get-me-out-of-here-now shriek of a fire alarm. Music is perhaps the most powerful sound of all, so think about how your music matches up with your sets and lighting. You want it all to work together to create the perfect mood. If you or a friend likes to edit music on the computer, you can always play around with adding sound effects. There are lots of free music editing programs out there to get you started.

Make a Mood

Arun has traveled around the world creating and touring lighting designs for dance and theater companies.

66 When I was a teenager, I loved playing with technology and lighting the shows at my high school. When I realized I could do this as my career, I started to work in professional theaters and learned how light was such a powerful tool in evoking reactions from the audience. Now, I get to play with high tech toys all day, and work with creative people on new shows all the time. 99

—*Arun Srinivasan*
LIGHTING DESIGNER

MAKING YOUR OWN COSTUME

Just as your personal style says something about you, costumes help tell an audience what your dance is all about. Marjorie knows this well—from giant mice to sugar plum fairies, she's created hundreds of outfits for dancers in the National Ballet of Canada. She's here to show us how, when it comes to making your own costumes, creativity is more important than money.

THINK VISUALLY

The costume designer translates the choreographer's general vibe (or vision for the dance) into clothes. Whether it's an old-school or futuristic look you want, begin by talking to the choreographer, watching the dance, and listening to the music. Don't worry if a complete vision doesn't immediately pop into your head. Instead, think about the look you're after—gather images, colors, and objects you think capture it, then sketch out your ideas.

FOUND IT!

A costume designer sees potential costume pieces around them all the time in everyday objects. Suddenly those twist ties can be sculpted into the perfect spiky hat, and aluminum foil is your new best friend. Start mixing and matching stuff in your own closet with sheets, towels, paper bags, or anything else you can transform. Just remember to ask first!

BE THRIFTY

A trip to the thrift store is a great and affordable way to get the pieces you're missing and to find new inspiration. Don't just look for that perfect jacket or pair of pants—think about how you can reuse things and piece them together in new ways. Love the fabric on that bag? Maybe you can cut it up and use it as a belt or headband.

DANCING MANNEQUINS

Remember, your dancers must be able to move about freely in your costumes. Think about how the fabric and shape of a piece of clothing will look and move on the dancers, and try to choose items that will accentuate the choreography. Heavier fabrics will be stiffer and hide movements more than light, flowing ones.

MAKE IT YOUR OWN

Try these ideas to finish off your costume creations:

· *Stencil it*—Design your own stencil with cardboard or a cereal box and start painting. A cool stencil on a T-shirt is one of the most effective and simple ways to make identical group costumes.

· *Trim it*—Trim is all the extra stuff that you can glue or sew onto your costume, like ribbons, buttons, or beads.

· *Paint it*—Use acrylic paint to add patterns or shapes to your costume. Try sponging it on for a textured look.

INSIDE *the*
PROFESSIONAL THEATER

OK, you're obviously not renting out an opera house for your first gig, but knowing the ins and outs of a professional theater can definitely help your show run smoothly, no matter what the venue.

1 STAGE DOOR

The performers and technicians get an instant backstage pass through this door, so the audience doesn't see them before the show starts.

2 DRESSING ROOMS

Everybody gets a mirror to do hair and makeup and get into costume. The rooms are usually decorated with good luck notes and bouquets of flowers.

3 THE GREEN ROOM

A (not necessarily green) room where performers can wait before going on stage. No one knows for sure, but it may have got its name because the color green calms the nerves, or because theater used to happen outside among the trees.

4 WARDROBE

Costumes are stored, washed, and maintained here.

5 THE WINGS

Where you get on and off stage, and where the technicians work. The rule here is "absolutely no talking," because the audience can hear you.

6 GRID

Technicians hang lights and pulley systems here high above the stage for lowering and raising elaborate set pieces.

7 STAGE

Where the magic happens. You guessed it, this is where you perform.

8 APRON

Not all stages have them, but it's any part of the stage that projects out into the audience.

9 HOUSE

Where the audience sits to watch the show. (This word is also used to describe the group itself, as in "it's a good house tonight.")

10 LOBBY

Guests enter the theater through the lobby, where they are greeted by ushers who hand out programs and help them to their seats.

11 BOX OFFICE

This is where the tickets are sold.

TECHIES TO THE RESCUE

You're all on stage and ready to go. Um, who's gonna hit play on the stereo? Time to call in the technicians! They're like theater ninjas, working in the shadowy world behind the curtains to make your show run smoothly. Look fast to catch them hanging like spiders, rigging pulleys from the ceiling, and whispering to each other through spy-like headsets.

Profile:

Nickname: Techie

Appearance: Dresses all in black to avoid being spotted by theater goers.

Mission: To cunningly deceive the audience with perfectly timed special effects.

Gadgets: Small flashlight, rope, and other household tools.

Powers and abilities: Stealth-like ability to be neither seen nor heard.

Personality trait: Loves the theater, but prefers staying behind the scenes.

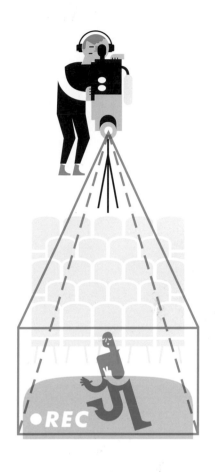

BACKSTAGE HEROES

Techies handle all the backstage stuff, like setting up and working the light and sound systems, moving sets and props around, handling special effects like fog machines, and making sure the dancers are where they should be at all times. Now matter how simple your show is, it's always good to have at least one techie around. Look for one among your friends, or even where you least expect it. Your little brother, perhaps?

CUE IT UP

The techie trick to making everything run effortlessly is the cue sheet. It's a list of all that needs to happen and in what order during the show. Stuff like opening the curtains, turning on the lights, or putting a prop on stage are all written down on the cue sheet. Once the show starts, the techies are in charge, so let them follow the cues and lead the way.

TIP: In professional theaters, the stage manager is the queen bee of all the technicians. She (or he!) calls all the "cues" and makes sure everything gets done at exactly the right time. Bottom line, it's good to have a boss backstage.

CAPTURE THE MEMORIES

After the show, you're going to want to look back on how it went, so put a second techie in charge of taping it all. Set up your camera at the back of the house so it captures the whole stage: No fancy zooming tricks! If you ever use the tape to remember the steps, you'll want to see what all the dancers are doing.

Attack of the BUTTERFLIES

This morning, you were full of anticipation, but now that the show's just a few moments away you feel more like you want to throw up. Before you run and hide, remember that nerves are a part of performing that everybody has to deal with, even the biggest stars. So how do you beat the butterflies and be able to rock your show?

PRE-SHOW WARMUP

Nothing is better at calming your nerves, or is more important than a good long warmup. Give yourself at least half an hour to wake up your muscles, loosen up, and find your balance. Ballet companies take a full class before a show because it's the best way to get your mind and body connected and focused on the performance. Once you're warm, try rehearsing, or "running through" a few of your steps.

FIND YOUR ZEN

Every dancer has a few tricks to calm themselves down. Give them a try if you're still stressing after your warmup:

· Find a quiet spot to lie/sit and meditate. Just breathe deeply and think relaxing thoughts.

· Try some yoga moves.

· Visualize yourself going through your dance and doing it all perfectly.

· Goof off and be silly. Turn up an energetic song in the dressing room and bounce around with your friends.

· Put it in perspective. Remind yourself that this is just one show, and whatever happens, it won't be the end of the world.

What Causes Nerves Anyway?

When you're nervous, your brain releases a bunch of chemicals that increase your heart rate and give you all sorts of extra energy—great if you need to fight off a bear. Unfortunately, our nervous system hasn't really caught up with our modern lives, so we're stuck with this crazy reaction, even to little stresses that aren't dangerous at all. But, nature's fix is pretty simple—slow, deep breathing is your body's way of saying to your brain "chill out, everything is fine." And it works!

Warmup Tip: One of those chemicals is adrenaline, which actually stops you from feeling pain. So don't go stretching way further than you usually do in your warmup, even if you think you're suddenly super rubbery. It's a mind trick, and you could really hurt yourself.

Performers can be really superstitious. They do crazy things for good luck, like wearing the same socks for an entire two-week run of a show. It seems bonkers, but they do it because in live theater, anything can happen. When you can't yell "cut" if something goes wrong, you really want luck on your side.

FAKING IT

When a prop rolls off the stage, or your costume rips, all you can do is keep on going. The golden rule is, fake it—act like nothing's wrong! If you accidentally fall down or get out of sync with the group, just improvise a few steps until you find your spot. Dance them as though it's your big solo moment, and then no one will know it was actually a slip-up.

DRESS REHEARSAL

The best way to avoid mistakes during a show is to get them all out of the way in the dress rehearsal. There's a dance superstition that a bad rehearsal equals a good show. It really just means it's important to get a few practice runs in with all the costumes and props. You'll inevitably have to make adjustments now that you're actually on the stage, like taking bigger steps to land all your formations.

BEFORE YOU HIT THE STAGE...

Do you have all the pieces of your costume? Don't forget your hat, and make sure you've taken off all your warmup clothes and jewelry!

· Is your hair and makeup in order? No smudges?

· Are all the props you need in the right place in the wings?

· Have you warmed up properly?

· Have you told your fellow dancers to "break a leg" (wished them good luck)?

TAKE A BOW

When you strike your last pose, your audience will want to thank you with applause. It's a classic rookie mistake to be caught in that moment, wanting to take a bow, and looking around at your fellow dancers, unsure what to do. Have a little something prepared in advance. It doesn't have to be elaborate, just something that matches your style.

CHAPTER 5

On the Scene

The video your buddy posted online this morning was so funny you nearly spit out your cereal. So you shared the link with all your friends. Before you head out the door, you throw on your vintage cartoon character T-shirt and grab your binder that's covered in stickers for your friend's new photography blog.

All these things give little hints to the world about who you are and the kind of stuff you're into. They also help more people find out about them, too. That's how garage bands eventually become supergroups, and how your friend's blog just might build up a global following.

What it all boils down to is this: if you're doing interesting stuff that people like, they'll want to tell their friends about it. So give them cool ways to do that! When it comes to promoting your shows, the more imaginative your ideas the better. Dance companies use everything from websites to coffee mugs to worn-out ballet shoes signed by dancers to promote themselves. One New York-based company called Dance Theater Workshop even asked their online followers to text in ideas that the company made in to dance moves. Very interactive!

Promoting your shows takes just as much creativity as making them, but that's what makes it so much fun. So whether it's making posters, blogging, or knitting your group's signature new leg warmers, start dreaming up fun ideas and watch your fan base grow.

Getting Your Name Out

Getting your message out means putting it in the right places. Just like gardening, you need to plant your "seeds" in spots where they will flourish. With some care and a little luck, your fan base will be growing in no time.

NAME THE SHOW

First things first, before you can start spreading the word, you need to have a word to spread. What are you gonna call your show anyway? If you've got lots of different groups performing, you need to find a show title that represents everyone. Find a theme and work it—maybe it's based on a dance style (like The Urban Dance Event?), your performance location (325 Gallery Dances), or something abstract that just conjures up a cool vibe (Tipping Points). When it's got that special ring, you'll know.

GET LISTED

People are always looking for fun things to do. Your local papers, community websites, and blogs help by posting event listings on everything from dog training classes to yoga in the park. These ad spots are almost always free, so be on the ball and submit your show info to them a few weeks in advance.

WORK THE SYSTEM

The pros hire professional PR people (as in public relations), who get their artists featured in magazines, newspapers, and on TV. You're not likely going to get an appearance on a talk show just yet, but you can take a lesson from PR people and look around for ways to get some extra promo. Get interviewed in the school newspaper, or ask your friend to write about you in a blog.

Release the Press

Before the internet, the only way to get some free promo was to get newspaper critics to write about your show. Today's dancers still strive to get a good review in the press. To make it happen, you've got to let those media types know about your show by emailing them a press release. Here's the basic format:

- · "For Immediate Release" goes at the top. (That's just industry speak for "something is happening right now that you should know about.")

- · Next comes your company name and contact info.

- · Insert a catchy title line ALL IN CAPS that entices media types to read more.

- · Write a blurb about how amazing your show is and how talented your people are.

- · Finish by giving out a contact email. Create one that's separate from your personal email, so you're not giving out any private information.

FOR IMMEDIATE RELEASE

The Next Best Thing Dance Company
Anytown
nextbest@example.com
(555) 555-5555

NEXT BEST PRESENTS BREAKING GROUND ON JAN 30 AT MAIN ST. AUDITORIUM

Breaking Ground is the fresh new show that's shaking things up and taking the dance world by storm. Come see what all the hype is about.

Media Contact: nextbest@example.com

POST IT!

I'll bet you've heard the saying "a picture is worth a thousand words." Words often fail when you're trying to describe your moves, and that's why so many dancers use photography to promote their shows. The good old dance poster is still the most popular marketing tool out there, and the best posters become works of art all on their own.

STEP ONE:
Taking Great Photos

A poster is only as good as its photo. Here are five tips for capturing the perfect shot.

1 Some cameras have a delay between when you hit the button and when the photo is taken. Figure out your camera's timing so you can nail those mid-air jumps.

2 Think about composition—how all the photo's pieces are put together. For example, if dancers are jumping, show the floor so we can see how high they are.

3 Avoid odd, distracting background objects. As in, "Is that pole coming out of the dancer's head?"

4 Flashes distract dancers. Instead, set your camera to a high shutter speed.

5 Don't over think things. Let go and roll with it—you'll get much better pics!

STEP TWO:
Crop & Craft It

Take that killer pic and use some photo-editing software to add special effects.

STEP THREE:
Basic Text

Don't clutter your poster with too much text. Give 'em the basics: your show name, date, time and location, and your website (or if you're advanced—and your parents agree—an email address for tickets).

STEP FOUR:
Print & Post

Put up your poster in all the places you think your fans might hang out—cool cafes, school bulletin boards, malls, or libraries. Just get the place's permission first!

Tip: If you've found a pic that captures your style perfectly, make good use of it. Work it into your company logo, or think about designing bookmarks, stickers, buttons, or anything else you can dream up.

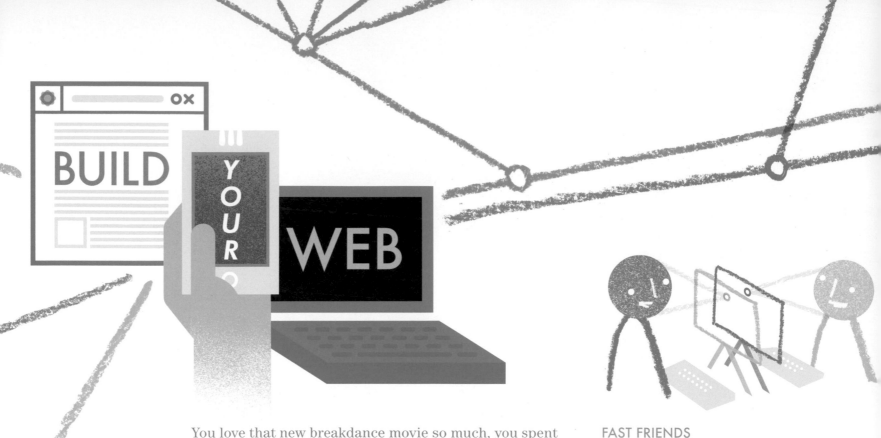

You love that new breakdance movie so much, you spent most of yesterday checking the fan sites and soaking up as much behind-the-scenes info as you could. When we really like something, we want to be a part of it. That's why websites and online networking are so popular—they make it possible for artists and fans to connect and communicate like never before.

FAST FRIENDS

The online world changes fast. Newer, cooler ways of connecting to people pop up all the time. It's amazing! It wasn't that long ago that the only way you could reach new fans was by spending oodles of money on radio or TV ads. These days, a clever video or blog post can go viral in minutes. All you have to do is come up with cool stuff to share, and suddenly you've got a fan base in Moscow. Sweet.

HOME ON THE WEB

Even with all the ways to share stuff online, having an old-fashioned website is still superior, because you can say it all in one centralized place. Start with the basics: a blurb describing what you're about, dancer bios, and a schedule of upcoming shows. Once that's covered, get creative by adding insider content like pictures, blog writings, video interviews and rehearsal clips. Post new stuff often to get fans coming back to your site.

WHAT TO SHARE?

Say it with me: "I will not spam my friends." Getting people's attention online isn't about bombarding their email and social network accounts with the same e-flyer. Trust me, that just makes people ruthless with the delete button. If you are writing an interesting blog, uploading cool videos, or generally making thoughtful comments online, the fans will find you (and then share your stuff with their friends). So tone down the group emails and just be the cool cat that you are.

IT'S A BIG CYBER WORLD

Just like in the real world, you need to be a bit careful and use your good judgment when strangers approach you online. Don't give out any personal information like your address, phone number, or school, and never agree to meet an online stranger that you don't know. If you get a weird feeling about someone, talk to your parents. They're actually pretty good with this sort of thing.

Moze Mossanen's Guide to
MAKING A DANCE VIDEO

Ever noticed that some of the best viral videos have dancing in them? From made-up silly dances caught on tape to that slick new music video, we just love 'em. Moze Mossanen, who's won several Gemini awards for his dance films featuring big-time choreographers, is here to show us that all you really need to make your own video is some great moves and a digital camera.

ON LOCATION

Filming a dance lets you play in ways that you just can't do live. You're not stuck on a stage in front of an audience, so start dreaming up some cool spots to film in. Want your dance to start in a classroom and then bust out onto the sidewalk? Awesome! Once you've found a great (and safe) location, you can switch up some of your moves so they fit perfectly. Maybe you start dancing while sitting at desks, or use some front steps to dance across different levels.

THE RIGHT ANGLE

Different shots, or camera angles, will give you more interesting choices when you edit everything together. Be sure to capture these four types of shots, even if you only have one camera. It just means you'll have to film everything a few times.

· *Wide Angle*—A nice big shot, where you can see all the dancers from head to toe.

· *Medium Angle*—A little closer, capturing one or a few dancers from head to waist or knee.

· *Close Up*—Zoom right in and film a dancer's head and shoulders.

· *Specialty Shots*—These shots are where you can get really creative. Follow your gut feeling about cool ways to film specific moves. Maybe you want to zoom in slowly during a solo, or move the camera quickly beside a dancer's running feet. Anything is possible!

PIECE IT TOGETHER

Editing is about putting together different shots in an interesting way. When you cut from one clip to the next, do it on an ending beat in the music or a spot where a movement naturally finishes before a new step begins. Here are the three stages of editing:

· *Assembly*—Start by putting your music track down, and drop in all the wide-angle shots with rough cuts where you want them.

· *Rough Cut*—Get a little fancier, playing around with different shots in different places. Once you like what you've got, show it to a few friends to get some honest feedback.

· *Fine Cut*—Make any final changes you want and you're done.

TIPS FOR THE DAY OF THE SHOOT

Make sure it's a nice bright day outside, or if you're filming inside, use a room with lots of windows. Ask a friend to act as a production assistant—the person who helps with everything from pressing play on the stereo to blocking pedestrians for two minutes while you film your sidewalk scene.

When it's all done, there's no bigger joy than sharing it with a group. So host a premiere—that's a party where you invite your friends and family to get together, watch your new film, and have some fun.

MOVING PICTURES

Dance is all about interesting moving imagery—no wonder it goes so well with film! Check out how these dances are enhanced through the magic of cinematography.

SECRET SERVICE
CHOREOGRAPHY: VICTOR QUIJADA, RUBBERBANDANCE

Romeo and Juliet's classical score never sounded so cool. In this break dance-meets-heist-film video, the story and dance are edited together for added drama.

MINT ROYALE
SINGING IN THE RAIN REMIX

Only the world of computer animation could turn this solo into a group dance. Who would have thought dancing piles of garbage would have such awesome moves?

DESCENT
CHOREOGRAPHY: NOEMIE LAFRANCE

Here, the top down camera angles help capture the interesting shape of the stairwell and the patterns the dancers make.

Making Connections

For all the amazing ways the internet connects us, there's still no replacement for actually meeting people face to face. All that blogging might be super fun, but the real payoff is when it leads to real life connections with other artists doing cool things. And the best part is, meeting these new friends is pretty much how you grow your career.

GET OUT THERE

In an artist's world, your dream job won't ever show up in the weekend classified ads. To land cool jobs, you've got to build up a reputation for making great dance. See shows, volunteer at cool festivals, and don't be too shy to let other artists know when you really like what they're doing. Your own moves will improve from watching others, and eventually you'll get that "Yes, I'd totally love to choreograph your band's music video" phone call.

INTRODUCE YOURSELF

Whether you're a major dance star trying to land a
show at a big-time theater, or a dance newbie wanting
to perform at your community festival, asking for a gig
is always intimidating. The pros do it by sending dance
presenters a press kit—a folder with some info on their
group, plus extras like news clippings, photos, and
video links. Muster your courage and send out your
own press kit. Your parents were right when they said
"it never hurts to try."

SECRET AGENT MAN

Eventually, you might be approached by a commercial
talent agent—a person who finds dance jobs for you in
TV and film, and in return, takes a part of the fee you'd
earn. Sounds cool, but be warned! Unfortunately, there
are a lot of scam agents out there, so you need to be
careful. If they guarantee you work or ask you to buy
things like lessons or photos to get started, just walk
away. Truth is, you can find most commercial audition
notices yourself—if film and TV is your thing, you
should do lots of research before choosing an agent.

Raise Some Funds

Your crew is dying to go to that weekend workshop with a top b-boy from NYC, but it costs a lot. And you'd love to upgrade your costumes, but don't know how you'll pay for it. At some point, having a little cash put aside can really help you take it to the next level. Now, a clever artist knows how to do things in style regardless of the budget, but they also know how to raise some funds when they need it.

PARTY WITH A PURPOSE

Do you throw a killer Halloween party each year that everybody talks about? Turn it into a fundraiser by charging a buck or two at the door, and you'll have your costume fund in no time. Add a raffle, a bake sale, or auction off some donated prizes to get even more bang for your buck. Creative types are particularly talented at throwing awesome, out-of-the-box fundraising events so have fun with it. Some of the coolest ideas I've seen are:

DANCE-O-GRAMS

Just like a singing telegram, how about surprising unsuspecting people on Halloween by selling mini Thriller dance performances?

DANCE MARATHON

This one's an oldie—raise money by getting a group together to dance for 24 hours straight. Be sure to trade off so everyone can get some rest breaks.

YOUR LIFE, DANCED

This choreographer auctioned off her talent, to make a dance inspired by the person who bid the highest. Hope the winner was interesting!

FOR THE RECORD

Get in the *Guinness Book of World Records* by organizing the longest line dance ever performed. Ambitious, yes, but people will reward you with pledges of support.

A LOVELY EXCHANGE

Gotta print up those programs and posters? Yikes, that's gonna cost you. Why not ask the printer to do the job for free, in exchange for an ad in your program? These kinds of mutually useful trades are called sponsorships, and if you find the right exchange, everyone's happy!

YOU WANT TO GIVE ME MONEY?

With a bit of research, you'll find that some organizations and foundations support young artists by giving out money as prizes, and grants which you can use to take classes, make dances, or put on shows. You usually have to fill out an application that explains how you'll use the money wisely. All in all, it feels great to win an award, and that bit of money can go a long way.

ARTFUL MANAGER

When it comes to group work, you're the one who takes charge, setting up an online calendar, handing out to-do lists, and making sure it all comes together on time. Your friends might call you a control freak, but I call you an arts manager!

There's a whole group of people working behind the scenes in dance doing cool stuff like running festivals, getting gigs for artists, or creating a buzz about a show. They're really important to the whole dance scene, because they help connect cool dance with new audiences. Here's what they do...

COMPANY MANAGERS

This is where the organization skills come in. Managers take an artist's big dreams and turn them into reality, one administrative task at a time. They do it all, from organizing rehearsal schedules and performances, to promoting upcoming events and hosting fundraisers.

PRESENTER

Also known as curators, these guys run a theater or a festival and spend lots of time watching shows, looking for groups they want to present. They work hard to build a scene of regular dance fans who come to all their shows, and they want to offer the best dance around.

Presenter Rush

It's called the "back of the house" moment—the excitement a presenter feels in a packed theater as the curtain goes up on the show they've organized. Magic!

66 When I was in school, I loved doing things like organizing concerts or booking bands to make our dances better. Now, it's my job! It's exciting to present world premieres, and I love discovering great dancers and bringing them to new audiences. 99

—Mimi Beck
PRESENTER, *DANCEWORKS*

ARCHIVIST

It's this person's job to collect and keep a record of dance events—stuff like programs, posters, videos, rehearsal notes, press clippings, interviews with dancers, and so on. It's like making a museum for future generations to look back on.

PUBLICIST

These people love to start a scene. They help create a buzz by getting your upcoming show in the press, sending out promo material and inviting VIPs to the show.

The way I see it, everybody should dance more! It's good for your body and even better for your imagination. But my favorite thing about dance is that it's like a good pal—and a smart one at that. Not only does it make every day a little more fun, it has helped me see the world around me in a different way. Over time, I started to see the world through dance, and even everyday things became a lot more interesting. I'd find choreography in the crowds at rush hour, or daydream up a spectacular dance number for my class to magically bust into during a boring lecture. It even got me curious about stuff I'd never thought about before. Like the science behind how my body works. Or learning about the history of the country that created that awesome music I can't stop dancing to. I never know where dance is going to take me next, and for me, that's the best part. Yeah, you get it—why walk through life, when you can dance?

FIND YOUR STYLE
Moves to Make Your Own

What does the dancer in you want to say, anyway? How do you find your dance "voice"? Well, learning about new styles is an awesome way to get started. Different kinds of moves will open your mind and help you discover your very own, one-of-a-kind dance voice. And where do you find these moves?

Point to anywhere on a world map, and chances are, you'll find a dance style to discover—each one with its own signature way of moving. Slow and graceful or fast and punchy, it's a dancing planet, and there are way too many styles to mention here. These ones show off some of the awesome variety out there,

and they're popular enough that'd you've probably heard of most of them.

This guide will tell you a little more about the personality of each style, and help you get going on your own dance path. Happy trails!

- African
- Ballet
- Ballroom & Salsa
- Belly Dance
- Bollywood

- Breakdance
- Broadway
- Contemporary
- Flamenco

AFRICAN
Moving Rhythm

The term "African" dance is actually a bit deceiving because of one super obvious geography fact: Africa is huge. It's got over 2,000 different languages and cultures (and as many dance styles to match). African dance usually refers to West Africa, but African dance teachers each have their own specialization (don't be shy to ask and learn!). No matter the exact style, traditional African dance serves up a high-energy rush that's better than any sugar high. You'll be sweating buckets with a smile as you dance to the beat of live drummers—a staple in any class.

Rhythm Sandwich

The drum, called a *djembe*, is like the heartbeat of the dance—it's where all the moves are born. Easy right? Except there are often lots of heartbeats happening at once! Confused? Technically, it's called polyrhythms—that's when several different rhythms are played at the same time. As a dancer, you interpret each rhythm with different parts of your body. Your arms may be dancing to one beat, while your legs follow another. Talk about concentration!

Try this: Bend your knees and lean forward slightly so your weight is over your toes and off your heels—just like a tennis player bounces while waiting for the ball. This stance will make sure you never miss the beat on any of those fast rhythms!

Tip: Traditional steps pull from everyday gestures—like casting out fishing nets or breaking down wheat—to tell a story or simply to celebrate life. But you're also encouraged to throw in your own moves, which keeps the style growing and changing all the time.

Tip: Don't forget your water bottle! OK, it's a really practical tip, but you're seriously going to need to drink lots and stay hydrated to keep up with this dance style.

BALLET
Swans of Steel

Ballet's all about poise and elegance. Sometimes, that gets it a bad rep as being a little uptight and stuffy. But look beyond the sugar plum stereotype. Behind every ballet dancer is the strength of a pro athlete, matched with the artistry to make it all look effortless. Ballerinas seem to float across the floor? Well, behind that illusion is lots and lots of muscle power!

Forceful Feet

One of the strongest parts of a ballet dancer's body is the feet. That's why ballerinas can stand on their toes for so long. Don't try that at home, because it takes many years to build up the muscle strength needed to go up "on pointe." And even then, you'll need a little help from specially fitted pointe shoes. They're not made of wood, as some people think, but with layers of thick material and glue, put together kind of like papier mâché. The shoe softens as you wear them. Some professionals go through a pair a performance!

Tip: Ballet has a lot of seemingly still poses. Make them come to life by imagining you're inside a large bubble and keep reaching for the edges of it—with your legs and feet, arms, head, and even your eyes.

Try this: Learn to "roll through your feet": Lift one heel up as high as you can, while keeping the ball of your foot and your toes on the floor (called "demi pointe"). Then keep rolling up, slowly peeling your toes off the floor until your toes are pointing down to the ground ("full pointe"). Roll back down reversing it all.

Tip: Focus on your transitions—the spots where you connect one step to the next. Make them blend together like gooey caramel to get that seamlessly elegant look you're after.

BALLROOM & SALSA
Cheek-to-Cheek & Head-to-Head

The ballroom world is not afraid of ramping things up. This ain't your grandma's Saturday night social dance anymore. Over the years, ballroom has developed an international network of dance competitions—called Dancesport—complete with rules, regulations and judges. There has even been a push to make Dancesport an official event at the summer Olympics.

Posture Police

Whether you're competing or not, ballroom is made up of many different dances, each with its own music and steps. There are "standard" dances (think Cinderella at the ball) and "Latin" styles, with faster feet and serious hip action.

All of these styles require the same proper posture and frame. That's the tall and broad shape your upper body and arms make while connecting to your partner. Posture is kind of like the skeleton for the dance—if it turns into spaghetti, there's no way to lead or follow your partner properly.

Try this: Stand with your back up against a wall and make sure the back of your head is touching it too. Now walk away from the wall, keeping that back position. Feeling regal? Good. That's how upright you'll need to stay as you dance!

Let Loose

Think of salsa dance as the free-spirited cousin of all the Latin dances. She's got the same fast feet and swinging hips, but she'd rather liven up a party than live by the Dancesport rules. That's why salsa dancers love to sprinkle in steps they've made up on the spot to show off their unique personalities.

Try this: This basic step will give you the framework you need to get going. It's just three moves, so try it out: Step forward, then back, then together joining your feet. Now with the other foot, this time going backward first: backward, forward, together. To get the rhythm, repeat: "Right-left-right-pause. Left-right-left-pause."

BELLY DANCE
The Hipsters

Belly dance is a pop culture name for traditional Middle Eastern dance. It got its nickname because of its fast, rhythmic hip movements, but there's a lot more to it than that. It's been around for thousands of years, and because it's so old, its origins are a bit of a mystery. It has roots in the Mediterranean, Middle East, and Egypt, but these days, it's hugely popular all over the world. You'll see it in movies and in music videos made by super-celebrities, like Shakira, Britney Spears, and Beyoncé.

Isolations

Belly dancing can feel a bit like rubbing your stomach and patting your head at the same time—complicated! That's because each body part does its own thing. It's called moving in isolation, and it means that your shoulders may be doing one thing, while your stomach or hips do another. It's a divide-and-conquer approach to dance that's as tricky for your brain as it is for your body.

Try this: Those famous hip moves are actually made by your legs. With your knees slightly relaxed, push one foot into the floor, straightening the leg until your hip naturally lifts a little bit. Then switch and try the other side. Now add your arms: As each hip goes up, bring that side's hand up next to your head to accent your face.

Expert tip: "The mystery of belly dance is that you use one body part to move another. For example, you move your legs to get hip actions, and your stomach to move your chest. The trick is to use the least amount of effort needed to make a movement happen. It's the opposite of ballet or jazz, where all your muscles are working all the time."

—*Yasmina Ramzy*
ARABESQUE DANCE COMPANY

Try this: Start by wobbling your knees back and forth—like fast, small alternating bends and stretches. Hold your arms out to the sides with your palms down, and relax the muscles around your stomach and hips until they start moving back and forth without any effort!

BOLLYWOOD
East Meets West

Bollywood is a nickname for India's film industry where, unlike Hollywood, the musical still rules as the most popular type of movie. Film producers compete to create bigger and better song and dance numbers, and it's paying off—the world can't get enough of Bollywood's over-the-top, upbeat style. People want in on the action, too—Bollywood dance classes are popping up all over the place.

Moving Tales

For these guys, it's all about the drama. Literally! In Bollywood dance, a lot of the moves and hand gestures are symbols for words like "come here," or "shame on you." So the dances actually show conversations between characters and help tell the story of the movie.

Expert tip: "Bollywood is a fusion of many styles. It helps to have a solid background in one classical Indian dance form so you'll understand the hand gestures and body positions. But it's also important to study all kinds of other styles so you can bring them into the mix."

—Lopa Sarkar,
BOLLYWOOD CHOREOGRAPHER AND TEACHER,
DIVINE HERITAGE ARTISTRY

Try this: One classic move is about showing off your bangles—the bracelets Bollywood dancers wear. To try it, lift your hands up on either side of your face and make fists. Twist your wrists back and forth, and look with your eyes to your right hand and then your left. That's how you say, "Aren't my bangles beautiful?"

Idea Exchange

Just like music videos, Bollywood moves are pop culture mash-ups of lots of different styles. They're definitely influenced by older styles of Indian classical and folk dance, but they'll happily take inspiration from other styles like jazz and belly dance, if it helps get the right look. The fun part is—the sharing goes both ways! Music video choreographers in the west borrow Bollywood moves too—like the Pussycat Dolls' "Jai Ho"—all in the name of entertainment!

Try this: One of the easiest staple moves in Bollywood dance is the shoulder shrug. Just hold your arms out to the sides with your palms up and elbows relaxed. Shrug your shoulders up and down to the beat, and smile while you're at it!

BREAKDANCE
Trend Setters

First things first—breakdance is a popular name for this style, but the dancers on the scene actually prefer to go by its original name—b-boying (or b-girling). Now hugely popular, b-boying began as part of New York City's hip-hop movement, along with deejaying, emceeing, and graffiti art. It got its aggressive style because b-boys used it, instead of violence, to battle out their problems.

Self Starters

It's part of the b-boy style to show off and make everything look easy, but there's tons of skill involved. You can't learn it all in a class either. Once you've mastered the basics, a big part of b-boying is coming up with your own style and moves. But what are those basics, anyway? Here's how they break down.

Toprock: Standing steps that get things going—your chance to find the beat and show off your own style.

Footwork/Downrock: Moves and patterns danced with both hands and feet on the floor.

Tricks/Freezes: Poses that take strength and balance to hold or "freeze" in for a while.

Powermoves: Just like it sounds—big, bold spinning moves like headspins and backspins.

Try this: Start with this footwork, and then play around with whatever arm and head moves you like. Step one foot out—either to the front, side, or back (your choice)—while opening your arms out to the side. Then step that foot back in, crossing your arms across your chest. Switch to the other foot, and just keep going. Add some bounce to your steps and just see what happens!

Expert tip: "When I'm dancing, I blast the music and start freestyling based on the vibe of the record. I find inspiration from the song's instruments, lyrics, and general message, or just the feeling I get when I take the track in."

—*Luther Brown*,
CHOREOGRAPHER, *SO YOU THINK YOU CAN DANCE CANADA*

BROADWAY
The Drama Queens

You probably didn't know it, but the song and dance numbers you see the *Glee* stars doing are a modern take on Broadway style. It's all about big moves, bigger voices, and lots of spectacle to wow the audience. Besides being a style of dance, Broadway is the name of the theater district in New York City. It's been the theater capitol of the world for close to a hundred years, and has given us two all-American dance styles: jazz and tap.

All That Jazz

Ever heard of jazz hands? Those snazzy fingers might not have the coolest reputation, but that's not the only look jazz has to offer. In fact, jazz dancers switch up their style all the time, depending on the look of the music theater production they're working on. Add a little breakdance, or maybe some acrobatics here—these dancers have got to be adaptable and ready to do it all!

Try this: Got a loud personality? Love trying new things? Then you'll love jazz. It's bold motto: "Go big or go home." You've got to use your face and eyes to help tell the story of the show, and always "dance to the back of the house." (Translation: exaggerate all your moves so even the person in the back row can see them.)

Expert tip: "To excel as a tap dancer, best to go for clarity of sound rather than speed. It's not about how fast you can dance but about the music you make with your feet."

—*Jessica Westermann*,
PROFESSIONAL TAP DANCER AND TEACHER

Try this: Get some noisy shoes and find a floor they'll click on. Start by standing on one foot (lean on the wall if you like). Brush the other foot forward and back, sliding the ball of your foot (where the toe tap would be) across the floor each time. Tap tap! Practice to build up your speed.

Make Some Noise

Tap dancers are rhythm obsessed. For them, the look of every step comes from the sounds it makes on the floor. Sometimes it's graceful, like in old Hollywood movies, but it also has a casual side, like in famous shows like *STOMP*. Whether their dance is light and airy, or heavy and grounded, tap dancers have amazing precision in their feet, and a musical mind.

CONTEMPORARY
What's New, What's Next?

Contemporary dancers are like the kids that wonder why they have to color between the lines. They'd rather have a blank canvas, and come up with new ways of moving that no one's ever tried before. Because it's all about thinking outside the box, it can look really different all the time. What binds it all together is really an idea or mind set about how to make dance, rather than a group of steps... Whoa, that's philosophical!

Challenge Assumptions

The name of the game is "question everything." Why do we have to dance to the music? Aren't "ugly" moves beautiful in their own way? It's all about looking at our beliefs about dance, and playing around with them. Like artistic explorers, contemporary dancers sometimes find amazing new dance discoveries.

Tip: Build up your confidence by taking classes from lots of different contemporary dance teachers. They'll each have their own style to show you, and it'll help you develop your ability to pick up new moves quickly.

Try this: Pick one move you see every day, and look closer. What's the most common way people walk. Are there differences in the way some people do it? Why? Then mix it up, just to see what happens. Can you reverse walk, or turn it inside out? Coming at a motion this way can open up all sorts of unexpected ideas for cool moves.

Rebellious Past

Contemporary dancers are following a long line of folks who liked to challenge authority—the modern dance scene that happened before the 1950s. This was a group of dancers who decided to break free from the strict rules of ballet. Eventually, some of those modern dancers became super-famous, like Martha Graham, who ironically created her own rules for dancing that people study all over the world.

Tip: Contemporary dancers don't wear shoes, so your feet will take a bit of a beating sometimes. Always keep some bandages and rolls of adhesive tape in your dance bag to deal with those unexpected scrapes.

FLAMENCO
Musical Conversations

Flamenco is a blend of strict control and wild abandonment. Picture the flamenco dancer with her straight, tall back and lifted head that stays perfectly poised while pounded out some intensely improvised leg and arm moves. How do they do it? It all comes out of the close relationship between the dancers and the musicians. They work together to create the passionate and proud performances they're famous for—kind of like having a conversation, but with music and movement cues instead of words. Each dance is unique, because the dancers and musicians "talk" to and feed off each other and see which way they want to take it all.

Making Music

The dancers are so connected to the music they even help make it—through stomping, clapping, and using castanets (small hand-held instruments that you click with your fingers). Some people call flamenco a "percussive" dance style, because, just like a drummer in a band, the rhythms the dancers create add complexity to the music.

Try this: Flamenco dancers have different ways of clapping that are used to get different sound effects. For a soft clap, or *palmas sorda*—cup your hands slightly as you clap and check out the muted sound. Compare that to *palmas claro*, or clear/strong claps, where you take three fingers of one hand and clap into the center of the other palm.

Expert tip: "Flamenco is the dance of your soul—it's about expressing who you are. Let your personality come through in your moves and have fun discovering yourself."

—*Esmeralda Enrique,*
ESMERALDA ENRIQUE SPANISH DANCE COMPANY

Index

A SPECIAL DANCE INDEX FOR YOU TO USE

On a Final Note: A few words of thanks: I'm so grateful to all the artists who contributed to this book: Tré Armstrong, Peggy Baker, Nova Bhattacharya, Luther Brown, Sean Cheesman, Esmeralda Enrique, Marjorie Fielding, Jean-Marc Généreux, Noémie Lafrance, Moze Mossanen, Heather Ogden, Meagan O'Shea, B-boy Luca "Lazylegz" Patuelli, Tara-Jean Popowich, Yasmina Ramzy, B-boy Drops (Jon Reid), Lopa Sarkar, Arun Srinivasan, Valerie Stanois, and Jessica Westermann. Special thanks to Cylla von Tiedemann for her dance photography tips, Megan Andrews and Susan Kendal at The Dance Current for connecting me with some great dance folks, Mimi Beck, Rosslyn Jacob Edwards and the Danceworks team, and Aviva Fleising at the Canadian Dance Assembly. Lastly, I'd like to sincerely thank John Crossingham for his endless enthusiasm and thoughtful editing, Jeff Kulak for the most beautiful illustrations, and Mary Beth Leatherdale for her ongoing insight and encouragement.